PRISONS

TROUBLED

SOCIETY

PRISONS

Renardo Barden

The Rourke Corporation, Inc.
Vero Beach, Florida 32964

The Rourke Corporation, Inc.
P.O. Box 3328, Vero Beach, FL 32964

Barden, Renardo.
    Prisons / by Renardo Barden.
       p. cm. — (Troubled society)
    Includes bibliographical references and index.
    Summary: Examines the American criminal justice system, conditions inside prisons, the rehabilitation of prisoners, and the future of prisons.
    ISBN 0-86593-110-0
    1. Criminology—United States—Juvenile literature. 2. Prisons—United States—Juvenile literature. [1. Criminology. 2. Prisons.] I. Title. II. Series.
HV6027.B37 1991
365.973—dc20   91-10843
                                                                                  CIP
                                                                                   AC

Series Editor: Gregory Lee
Editors: Elizabeth Sirimarco, Marguerite Aronowitz
Book design and production: The Creative Spark,
    Capistrano Beach, CA
Cover photograph: Hank Morgan/Photo Researchers, Inc.

Contents

ONE

CRIME IN AMERICA

If you were homeless and living on the streets of a big city without a warm coat, you would suffer from the cold. Lacking money, you would be hungry and dogged by weakness. Stronger people might beat you up just for your shoes. If you were abusing alcohol, sooner or later you would become very sick and require medical attention. If you were doing drugs, your life would be in constant danger from dealers and users.

You might be standing on a dark street and see as many as 100 wristwatches in a shop window. A rock thrown through the glass would allow you to stuff your pockets with the timepieces and run off. The watches could be sold. With the money, you could rent a heated room with a bed. You could buy nourishing meals in restaurants, get liquor or drugs, and be safe for a while from threats of violence.

But if police saw you crossing the street, called you over to the car and found all the stolen watches in your pockets, what then?

You would probably be charged with stealing the watches, arrested, and taken to jail. The watches would be seized as evidence to be used at your trial. You would probably be locked up—at least for a while.

Next, you would be *arraigned*. That is, you would be taken before a judge who would explain the charges against you. At that time you would be given a chance to plead guilty or not guilty. A court-appointed lawyer would advise you, if you could not afford your own.

You might plead "guilty" and waive your right to

At the start of the 1990s more than one million men and women were in prisons and jails throughout the United States. Two percent of the U.S. population is behind bars, on parole, or on probation.

a trial. In that case, the judge would decide whether to put you on *probation*, a form of legal supervision when the court keeps track of your actions. Or the judge may sentence you to jail or prison. If you pleaded "not guilty," a time and date would be set for your trial. Because there are always more cases to be tried than judges to try them, your trial would be set several weeks in the future.

Knowing that you are homeless, police would attempt to keep you locked up. But city jails are often too crowded to hold all the people accused of committing a crime. So, as has happened recently in Portland, Oregon, and other communities, the police might have to let you go. In that case, you would have to sign a piece of paper promising to appear for trial, and then you would be free to leave. Even if you pled guilty to theft of the watches, police might let you go because there isn't enough room to keep you. The courts have forbidden subjecting human prisoners to overcrowded conditions because the Constitution forbids "cruel and unusual punishment." Overcrowding is certainly cruel. How would you like to sleep on the cement floor of a cell with a toilet bowl for a pillow?

Of course, releasing prisoners for lack of space doesn't happen all the time, and releasing suspected and convicted offenders from jail is still fairly rare. As you might guess, many who are released never show up for their trials.

Suppose you had not been released? What if you had been tried and found guilty? If stealing the watches was a first offense, you could expect a measure of mercy. Perhaps you would be sentenced to serve 90 days in jail. A severe sentence? Maybe not. Remember, before you stole the watches you were homeless. Now you would have a bed, a full stomach, a measure of warmth, and a regular—if regimented—life. You might even be able to get some free dental work from the prison dentist! So, looking at the situation from another perspective, stealing the watches and being caught might lead to a life only slightly less pleasant than one you were trying to achieve with the stolen watches.

Crime Doesn't Pay—Or Does It?

In America today the old saying, "crime doesn't pay" does not always hold true. It would be safer to say that some crimes rarely pay, and some often do.

America has a soaring crime rate. Guns and drugs virtually rule many city neighborhoods. Politicians and police talk of the "war on drugs" and "getting tough on crime." But this policy is expensive, especially when—as it turns out—getting tough on crime consists only of putting people in prison.

To respond to the rising crime rate with prison sentences, authorities have raised taxes and cut back on other vital services such as public transportation, education, child care, health care and welfare. With the increased tax money, authorities have recruited more police, agents, and guards. They have built more courtrooms and prisons, appointed more judges, and retained more attorneys to prosecute and defend more criminal suspects. Yet American prisons are still bulging from the load.

In the middle 1970s, when large numbers of politicians began calling for a tougher approach to drug use and social disorder, about 200,000 Americans were in jail. The view at that time was that a more severe response to crime would cause criminals to obey the law. The crime rate was expected to drop. But it didn't work out that way.

Today, approximately one million Americans are behind bars. And despite recently reported decreases in some crimes, the overall crime rate remains about the same. More alarmingly, violent crime is still climbing. The United States leads the world in the number of citizens imprisoned.

Yet as we build new prisons and hire more police and prison guards, many of our cities are setting another kind of record. Fifteen American cities—including New York City—set all-time records for the number of murders in 1990.

The problem of whether there are enough prisons sometimes has a twist. Not long ago, New York City Criminal Court Judge Michael A. Gross told a reporter that accused criminals sometimes seek longer sentences than they are given. Gross said he usually refuses to honor the requests: "The courts are not a social service agency. The criminal justice system is designed to provide punishment, not housing."

In one way, Gross is right. But in reality, the criminal justice system sometimes ends up protecting and sheltering criminals from a worse life on the streets.

Consider Stepfon Wilkins, a 27-year-old man locked up not long ago in the Manhattan Detention Complex, a New York City jail known as the

Guards keep watch at the Mack Alford Correctional Center in Oklahoma.

"Tombs." Wilkins had many reasons for preferring life in jail to life in a city shelter for homeless people or living on the streets.

"I have my own little room," he said, describing his routine at the Tombs. "In the shelter there's a whole floor with a hundred and eighty, two hundred beds. It's a little safer here, too. In jail all you can get is a razor if you want to start a fight. In the shelters people get guns. In the shelters the food is second rate. By the time it gets to you it's cold. The bread is stale. Here, it is fresh and hot."

Wilkins had been accused of receiving stolen property, a minor crime. He had not killed or injured

Waiting For Trial

What follows is a real-life account of a young man under arrest for burglary. David Kendig (not his real name) tells this story in his own words, which have not been changed.

L.A. County Jail was a nightmare. It usually takes anywhere from five to 20 hours to just get admitted. All through this time you are shuffled from holding cell to holding cell, which are made for 25 to 30 men and they put anywhere from 50 to 100 men in them. Wall to wall people standing, sitting or lying shoulder to shoulder. Anyone from the murderer to the drunk driver to the person with too many tickets are all thrown in together...

After you are finally processed in, finger-printed, picture taken, and fed your cheese sandwich and koolaid, you are taken to a dorm that is supposed to hold 500, but they put up to 1,000 men in. Mattresses all over the floor, wall to wall men who have just been through hell to get to this point. The guards tell you that you must stay awake in order to hear your name, to be brought to another dorm or cell.

I was brought to a six-man cell that they had nine [men] sleeping in. The overcrowded conditions are incredible. As I see it, you can only pack so many people into a space before it explodes. There were fights, beatings, robbings, and the cops giving flashlight therapy every day....

—*David Kendig*

anyone, and he wasn't dealing drugs. Therefore, he was eligible for a stay in New York's "easiest" jail. In the Tombs, Wilkins enjoyed access to a weight room where he could work out. Like other inmates he was allowed to leave his cell and watch color television.

People like Wilkins who prefer life behind bars often make society feel uneasy and frustrated. It's tempting to say that the Tombs should be made more unpleasant so Wilkins and those like him will prefer life on the streets. But there are good reasons this would not be the right thing to do.

First, the American Constitution forbids "cruel and unusual" punishment. Second, it is necessary for us to understand the limits of punishment—where punishment leaves off and cruelty begins. Finally, our way of life is based on a commitment to government by written law. To increase the punishment of some prisoners and spare others who have been convicted of the same offense violates both a sense of fairness and the rules of the Constitution.

Necessity Versus Cost

The fact that someone like Wilkins prefers jail to life on the streets raises another issue. Why was he living on the streets? Does he have a drug or alcohol problem? Was he abused as a child? Could a better education, more love, comfort, respect, and money have made a difference in his behavior? In other words, should society spend more on locking up the problem, or taking preventative measures?

These questions are necessary to ask if we are ever to resolve the crisis in our prisons and improve the workings of our justice system.

This is a holding cell in the Travis County, Texas, juvenile detention center.

If the answer is yes, that Wilkins' life was harmed by factors he could not control, perhaps we should consider whether or not we are asking too much of our jails and prisons. Are our jails being asked to make up for bad parenting, lack of job opportunities, poor medical and emotional care, and inadequate education? Is society asking punishment to do what it cannot? If the answer is no, that obeying the law is a matter of personal responsibility no matter what ails us, then prisons are still a necessary part of maintaining law and order.

If we hired more teachers today, could we save money by hiring fewer police tomorrow? If we paid more money for child care so parents could work at good jobs and children could have contact with people who cared for them, would we save money by building fewer prisons over the next several years?

Imprisoning people is incredibly expensive. To build a single prison cell, for example, costs about $75,000. This is just for one small, dark, locked room. To feed, clothe, and provide medical care for a prisoner for one year costs another $30,000. And since most criminals are in the parenting years of their lives, their children must often be cared for at society's expense.

Crime in America continues to be a spiraling problem with no end in sight. How we deal with criminals once they are caught is yet another endless problem.

TWO

THE CRIMINAL JUSTICE SYSTEM

The criminal justice system was created to handle those accused of committing crimes.

Crimes are usually divided into two categories: *misdemeanors* are minor offenses; *felonies* are more serious crimes.

When a crime is committed, police first seek evidence about the offense and the offender, arrest the offender, then bring him or her before a judge.

If the offense is not terribly serious (a misdemeanor, or if the offender is young with no criminal record), the judge may offer what is known as *diversion*. In criminal justice, diversion is the opportunity to avoid being tried for the offense. In return, the offender usually agrees to seek help with drug or alcohol problems, perform community service, or repair or make restitution for the offense.

If diversion is not offered, and the suspect is tried for the crime, he or she is entitled to certain legal rights. First, the law holds that the accused is presumed innocent until proven guilty. Second, the suspect is entitled to be represented by an attorney and to be tried by a jury of peers (fellow citizens). Juries are selected for specific trials from available pools of prospective jurors.

The trial occurs in a courtroom presided over by another judge. Prosecuting attorneys are responsible for presenting evidence intended to prove the guilt of the accused. Defense attorneys try to persuade the court that the person is innocent. The judge referees among the attorneys, rules on their arguments, and clarifies legal points so the jury

A prison law library. Many inmates study the law in order to work on their own court appeals.

understands the trial.

In a trial, the burden of proof is on the prosecution. Prosecuting attorneys must establish "beyond a reasonable doubt" that the accused really committed the crime or crimes. When a jury is not convinced, the accused is found not guilty and released from custody.

If a jury finds the suspect guilty, the judge must decide on how to punish the offender. In doing so, a judge will consider the seriousness of the offense, the danger posed to society by the offender, as well as the offender's age and prior criminal and arrest record. In some instances, particularly those involving drugs and repeat offenders, the judge must follow sentencing guidelines and hand out a prison sentence of a specific length of time. Otherwise, the judge is allowed to use personal judgment.

Although the relationships of one court to another can be complex, one of the functions of the "higher" courts is to consider *appeals*. A convicted offender retains the right to appeal the conviction. In other words, he or she can have the events surrounding the earlier trial considered by a higher court. An appeal is a request to remove a case from a lower court to a higher court. It can result in the higher court overturning the conviction of the lower court and releasing the offender from custody.

The Suspended Sentence

The judge may give a *suspended sentence*, where the offender does not have to serve time in jail provided he or she does not get into trouble again.

The judge may also decide to sentence the offender to a period of probation. Under typical probation terms (six months, a year, or a longer period) a convicted offender is under a form of community supervision—with conditions.

Probation may require that an offender avoid drinking and drugs. It may require that he or she continue to live in the community and not move from the area. It may require avoiding certain people. And it almost certainly will require reporting to a probation officer on a regular basis. While on probation, an offender can work at a paying job, live with his or her family, and enjoy a somewhat normal

The Hearing Process

From the cell or dorm you go to court, which is more holding cells, sitting for hours until you're called into a courtroom for five minutes and told that a public defender will see you. After you're assigned a public defender who already has at least ten other cases, you are either brought back into the courtroom if there is time, or brought back to county jail and another court date is set for you. That could be anywhere from the next day to three weeks.

If you're not fighting your case and just plead guilty you can be out of the court system in three or four months...if you decide to fight your case it can take a year to years of going in and out of court and back to the county jail. Most cases if they see that you are going to take it to jury trial, the DA [district attorney] will try to cut some kind of deal, so they don't have to pay for a jury and court costs. Whatever happens, you don't really have that much to say about your case. You are told to shut up and listen to what the judge says, which at the time you are in the courtroom is hard to remember because of the little amount of time and all the legal jargon....

—*David Kendig*

life. Should the offender violate the terms of probation, however, he or she can be sent to jail or prison.

Juveniles

The law defines offenders younger than 18 as *juveniles*. Juveniles are usually given more lenient punishment than adults who commit the same crimes. Some states have laws establishing maximum periods of confinement for those under age 18. Gang members in California and elsewhere have been known to take advantage of such laws by recruiting very young people to commit murder. Murder, an offense that could well result in the death penalty or in life imprisonment for an adult, may draw only a couple of years for a juvenile.

When necessary, young offenders are usually locked up in juvenile halls or detention centers. Supervision and guidance are usually emphasized in these facilities. Lockups and solitary confinement are normally reserved for adult prisoners.

There are several thousand jails and local detention facilities for juveniles and adults who have committed misdemeanors in the United States. There are also about 250 major juvenile facilities and approximately 600 adult prisons. Adult prisons differ from one another in many ways. Convicted criminals are usually classified by authorities and sent to a prison most suited to offenders of their classification.

Jails

A jail is a community- or city-operated facility where suspected criminals are held after being arrested and before coming to trial for a crime.

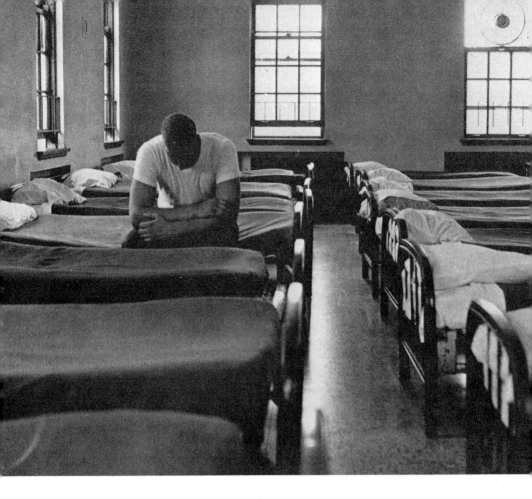

This dormitory is at the State Correctional Facility for Youth in Red Wing, Minnesota. These are places of minimum security for young people who, it is hoped, will not break the law again.

Sometimes jails are used to house convicted offenders, but usually only if their sentences are short. Convicted offenders with more than a few months to serve are usually sent to prisons.

Prisons

Maximum-security prisons are usually surrounded by walls and double fences. Observation towers are positioned so guards can monitor inmates approaching the fences and walls. These towers

THREE

THE PURPOSE OF IMPRISONMENT

People with the disease of epilepsy sometimes experience sudden and violent episodes. These seizures are often called "fits." Epilepsy once was considered a sign that the sufferer was possessed by a devil or an evil spirit. Epileptics were often shunned, injured or killed. But today epilepsy is controlled with medication. Similarly, thousands who once would have been called insane and locked up in asylums are leading normal and productive lives, thanks to determined people who asked the right questions and refused to pass moral judgments on those afflicted.

Criminologists with a background in psychology and science often talk about the *treatment model*. The word "treatment" refers to medical or scientific help. The word "model" means a small, ideal version of an object or theory. The treatment model asks us to consider what we might learn by looking at crime as a social disease. If epilepsy and mental depression can be relieved with medication; if alcoholism and drug addiction can be eased with medical and psychological care; what about criminal behavior? Can crime be treated scientifically and its effects lessened?

In recent years, scientists have gathered evidence that shows a tendency—or weakness—toward alcoholism and drug abuse may be inherited. Since much crime is committed by people who have substance abuse problems, these areas of investigation are important to society. Research also suggests that

More than 80 percent of all state and federal prisoners are recidivists—that is, inmates who have committed crimes after serving a previous prison term or being on probation.

antisocial behavior that leads to crime may be inherited. Does this mean that crime may someday become treatable in a medical sense? Yes, it may mean just that. It does not mean, however, that prisons will become unnecessary or that we should give up on imprisonment as a social policy. The safety of all citizens is important. Some form of imprisonment or restraint will always be necessary.

Some 30 years ago researchers analyzed more

than 48 different societies around the world. They learned that those who do not punish crime or anti-social behavior have difficulty maintaining full-time spiritual leaders, teachers, and administrators. Historically, then, human societies have always required some form of punishment for antisocial behavior.

There are many ways of punishing people. What makes prison an effective method of punishment? What do we expect our prisons to accomplish with prisoners?

Punishment And Restraint

Prisons punish by denying freedom, and imposing rigid timetables on prison inmates. But prisons are very expensive to build and maintain. Could the taxpayers' money be put to better use by coming up with other forms of punishment?

What if we returned to the early practice of flogging (public whipping), or putting people in public stocks? If flogging again became an accepted form of punishment, money saved by not imprisoning the offender might be given to the victims of the crime instead. But then the criminal would be out on the street again. The public stock method locks a criminal by the ankles and wrists in a wooden frame. Anyone who wants to can come by and see the criminal publicly disgraced. Maybe some criminals would prefer prison, where they cannot be seen, to embarrassing exposure in public.

To most of the public, the most important function of a prison is to provide restraint. Prisons temporarily prevent criminals from committing more crimes. A person locked up will not be robbing another liquor store or committing another rape. But is restraint enough?

Rehabilitation And Deterrence

Criminals are not restrained from committing crimes while they are in jail. Sometimes they corrupt prison guards, or take advantage of prisoners who are young, weak, sick or elderly. Criminologists, judges, guards and many others know that prisons are training camps for crime. The harshness of prison life usually makes inmates bitter, and they are often more angry with the human race when they are released than when they went in.

To *rehabilitate* inmates is to educate them to change their behavior. Ideally, they are taught to value the pleasure of liberty and responsibility, and to prepare for life outside the walls. Until recently, rehabilitation was an expressed goal of all United States prisons. But rehabilitation is an uncertain process that differs from one individual to another.

Rehabilitation is the most expensive part of prison policy, because it often calls for counseling or therapy as well as job training. On the other hand, if a prisoner never goes back to jail, the extra expense is worthwhile. Unfortunately, we are often unwilling to spend the needed money to try to rehabilitate offenders. Prison riots have also helped discourage public interest in rehabilitation. The very idea of rehabilitation was recently written out of the California Penal Code.

According to psychologists, rewards are more likely than punishment to produce new behavior.

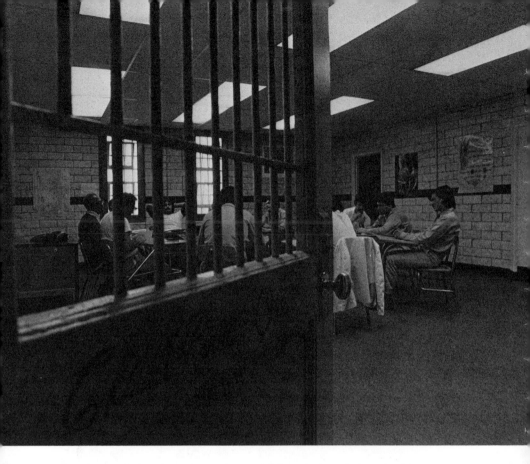

One of the ways the prison system tries to rehabilitate is through classes to improve an inmate's education, like this one in a Rhode Island correctional institution.

This does not mean that society should reward criminals—rather that punishment is probably too slow and too unreliable a method to change criminal behavior. Not only are most criminals never captured, tried, and imprisoned, but the time that elapses between the crime and the punishment is often long.

Punishment, however, is the method most societies choose to try to change criminal behavior. This method is called *deterrence.* The effects of deterrence are hard to measure, however, because human beings differ so much from one another. The threat of being punished may be more vivid to some people than to others. And for some, the risk of getting caught seems to sweeten the offense. In other words, one person's deterrence may be another person's "challenge."

There are two types of deterrence: general and specific. Specific deterrence refers to an individual, a crime, and a penalty. For example, the robber decides not to hold up a liquor store to avoid another prison term. But think again of Wilkins, for whom being in jail is no big deal. It comes as no surprise then that prisons eventually lose much of their specific deterrent value. The result is called *recidivism*. Recidivism is the tendency of inmates to return to prison again and again.

Criminologists think that prisons are best at general deterrence. General deterrence means the existence of prisons prevents people who have never been to prison from committing crimes.

A Glimpse Of Prison Life

Maximum-security prisons differ from medium- and minimum-security institutions. Likewise, prisons in one state usually differ somewhat from those in another. Conditions in federal prisons differ from state prisons, city jails, halfway houses, and juvenile halls. There are, however, things that all prisons have in common.

Because prisons are generally underfinanced and understaffed, they rely heavily on routine. Plain but nourishing meals are served at the same times every day, and inmates assigned work tasks do them at the same time and in the same way every day. Times are also routinely assigned for showers,

Life Behind Bars

The worst thing you can be in jail or prison is a "rat," someone that tells the cops on other inmates...A lot of the fighting that is done in prisons is done with "shanks"—homemade knives that can be made out of almost anything that can be sharpened to a point. Hits or assassinations are done...over almost anything...

You can be sent to the hole, a one-man cell where you have nothing but the bed, toilet and yourself. You are showered twice a week and get rec yard every two days—if you're lucky...

I also found out that there are a lot of drugs in prison—weed, coke, speed, heroin. Most is brought in by visits...since there is no cash money in prison, the dope is paid for by trade at canteen or a thing called "call-outs." One inmate calls his people on the street and has them send a money order to the inmate with the dope, or to his people on the street.

—*David Kendig*

medical appointments, library use, canteen visits, and outdoor recreation.

Depending on the prison and cell sizes, inmates either have their own cells or share space with cellmates. Depending on security conditions, inmates eat their meals alone, with their cellmates, or in cafeterias with many inmates.

Security needs, discipline, and inmate behavior also determine the amount and kind of recreation offered in prison. Prisoners are ordinarily allowed outside into enclosed yards once or twice a day. There they may visit with one another, smoke cigarettes, seek news of friends and families, and share plans and hopes for the future.

But the yards can also be dangerous. Suspected snitches are often beaten or stabbed. Since the prisoner code forbids snitching, and since the yards are crowded, it is often difficult for authorities to watch everything that's going on. When something like this happens, prison authorities may "lock down" or discipline entire cellblocks. Groups of inmates are locked into their cells for specified periods of time. Discipline can also include suspension of yard time and no television.

Most prisons have canteens where prisoners are able to buy cigarettes, candy, postage stamps, stationery, small food items, and other luxuries the prison does not provide. Money to shop at these canteens comes either from relatives who deposit money into the prisoner's canteen account, or from small wages usually paid prisoners who are qualified to work. Generally, prisoners are forbidden to have cash in their possession at any time. Money is held

Making automobile license plates in a prison shop. Inmates can earn small sums of money at such jobs, using their wages to pay for personal items in the prison store or "canteen."

on account by the prison or transferred to the canteen where it may be spent in limited ways.

For most inmates, their major problem is how to spend time. Most prisons have some recreational outlets such as gyms where prisoners can lift weights and train; libraries where they can read or do legal research; and even shops where they learn welding, auto mechanics, or some other trade. But there is always more time than there are activities to fill it. As a result, prisoners often turn to some form of crime as they serve out their sentences.

Crime In Prison

Prisons are like small societies. In this case, they are societies made up of people who have been convicted of breaking the law. Not surprisingly, criminal problems found on city streets also exist in prison.

Drugs, while harder to obtain in prison, do exist and regularly change hands in prison. Often the cash part of the deal is handled by relatives or friends outside the prison. How do drugs get in? Sometimes they are sneaked in by relatives. Sometimes they are brought in by the prison guards in exchange for cash.

Violence is another crime that occurs in prison. Snitches are targets for violating prisoner codes. Gangs thrive in prison, and many inmates band together by race or ethnic type to offer each other protection. Sometimes prisoners fight over privileges.

Another of the many problems prisons have to deal with is lack of sexual contact for men. Homosexual relationships often occur as a result of this all-male isolation. Increasingly, prison authorities have found that it is easier to keep the peace if inmates are allowed occasional *conjugal visits* with their wives or girlfriends. They are viewed as a reward for good behavior, however, and sometimes are taken away for disciplinary reasons. These conjugal privileges do not exist in all prisons.

FOUR

A HISTORY OF IMPRISONMENT

Prisons arose from society's need to keep order in a sometimes violent world. Prisons have ranged from simple holes dug in the earth, to castle towers, to modern maximum-security prisons that house thousands of inmates and resemble small cities.

The earliest prisons were not places of prolonged confinement. They were places where people were locked up until the authorities decided to torture, execute, free, or banish them. Sometimes people were shut up in prisons and left there to die. Often people were sent to prison for the "crime" of being unpopular with those in power. In some parts of the world even today, this has not changed.

Most early prisons were not established to punish criminals. For example, one of the first was Bridewell, an English palace that once belonged to King Edward IV. It became a "workhouse for the poor and idle people" in the 16th century. Rural poor were given food and shelter in exchange for work, but they had to work very hard for every morsel of food. In a short time, Bridewell became a profitable business. Before long, "workhouses" spread throughout England and northern Europe. They were created mostly to force the poor to work and lead orderly lives that could be made profitable—if not for the poor, then for those who operated the workhouses.

Minor criminals and common thieves were often locked up in dark, overcrowded buildings where they were left to sicken and die. Wrongdoers were tortured. Serious offenders were put to death at

A debtor's prison in 18th century England, where entire families were locked up if the head of the household owed money to others.

public spectacles. Typically such people were hanged or burned at the stake. These gruesome displays were a popular form of entertainment—like a horror movie, except that the horror was real. Those who administered such punishments hoped they would deter other people from crime.

Banishment And Transportation

Often there were political or religious reasons for sparing offenders, especially if they were members of royal families or the clergy. The punishment for these people was often *banishment*. They were sent far away from their homes and never allowed to return.

By the 17th century, England had established colonies all over the world that were run as businesses for the profit of the English. Almost always the colonies suffered from a shortage of labor.

To remedy this lack of workers, the English began a policy called *transportation*, the shipping of wrongdoers or undesirable people to the colonies— particularly America and Australia. Prisoners could be made to work as slaves until their sentences expired or they died. Over the years, thousands of convicts were shipped to America (and later Australia) in chains. Some people also came voluntarily to avoid being imprisoned for debt in England.

Debt has always been one of the leading causes of imprisonment. "Debtors' prisons" were popular institutions in Europe, and especially in Great Britain. A reform movement swept through America in the 1830s, however, and today Americans are no longer imprisoned just for owing money.

The Enlightenment

The concept of prisons as places of rehabilitation had to await the spread of ideas coming out of the historical period known as the Enlightenment. During the 18th century, education and knowledge came to be valued by many more people.

A Frenchman named Montesquieu argued that the law ought to strive to create social justice. He said that anger had no role in the administering

of law, and held that harsh punishments were unciv-
ilized. Montesquieu also favored separating those
who wrote laws from those who enforced them. The
American system of law does this by separating the
legislative and judicial branches of government.

In 1764, an Italian named Cesare Beccaria
published one of the most important documents in
the history of criminal justice. *An Essay on Crimes
and Punishment* advanced many new ideas.
Beccaria held that preventing crime is more important than punishing it. He said that punishment
should be equal to the crime, and opposed those
who would use the law for revenge. Beccaria influ-
enced the writers of the Constitution of the United
States. Many of his basic principles have become a
part of the Bill of Rights (the first ten amendments to
the Constitution). Among these principles are the following:

- The accused should be held innocent until proven
  guilty.
- The accused should not be forced to testify against
  himself.
- The accused should have the right to legal counsel
  and to cross-examine witnesses brought
  against him.
- The accused should have the right to a prompt
  and speedy trial by jury.

The Walnut Street Jail

In early America, William Penn established a
series of liberal laws in the colony that would
become the state of Pennsylvania. Penn wanted to
abolish the death penalty except in cases of murder.

The word *penitentiary*—a prison—comes from the word *penitent,* meaning a person who regrets a sin or offense.

When America had became independent (after Penn's death), a group of his followers who called themselves the "Philadelphia Society for Alleviating the Miseries of Public Prisons" took over a part of the Philadelphia city jail, known as the Walnut Street Jail. There they established prison industries, provided basic medical services, and attempted to educate the inmates. Hardened criminals were separated from younger offenders for the first time.

True to Penn's Quaker philosophy, the Society emphasized individual conscience and the value of solitude. The jail relied heavily on solitary confinement, as the Society believed that prisoners would repent more readily if they observed strict silence and were kept apart. Soon other prisons began imitating the Walnut Street Jail model.

Some people, however, thought the Walnut Street Jail was too severe. They argued that lives of silence and idleness led to madness as often as personal reform.

The New York State Prison at Auburn, New York, opened in 1819. Officials there were determined to do away with what they saw as the evils of the Pennsylvania system. At Auburn, inmates were still locked up in small, solitary cells by night, but required to work during the day. Auburn's architecture—long rows of cells attached to a large administration building—became the physical model for most new prisons.

The Indeterminate Sentence

In 1840, Alexander Maconochie was appointed

The Easy Life?

The reason I feel that there is such a great return rate in prison is that it is so bad out there on the streets—and a pretty easy life in here. We have no responsibilities.

Guys have their homeboys or buddies in here, you work your little job and then there's nothing that you really have to do. Free meals, medical, dental. Most of the time you have someone out there sending you money or packages. You don't have to deal with wife or family unless they come visit you, and then you are the center of attention.

Most men in here have nothing to look forward to on the outside. Sure, everyone talks about getting out but they also talk about coming right back in here. When you're on parole you use drugs, sell drugs, or commit another crime and get caught, nine times out of ten, all you're going to get is a violation, six months to a year. So you end up doing three to six months, or if you're a violator without half time you do the full term you are given. Either way that's enough time to clean up, get healthy and hang out with the fellas for a while...even though we are locked up there are men in here who have learned how to do time and don't care if they're put back in here time and again. That is one of the main reasons it is so overcrowded in prisons and jails. Many men have much better lives in here than they do on the street.

—*David Kendig*

to operate a British penal colony in Australia. To improve conditions at this grim place, he developed the "mark" system, where a prisoner's good behavior was rewarded by a shortened sentence. A prisoner gradually earned the right to work with others, and was even allowed to decide how much and what kind of work he would undertake (which helped determine how rapidly he would progress toward earning his freedom).

Maconochie's ideas were gradually taken up by the Irish penologist Sir Walter Crofton. Under Crofton, the indeterminate sentence became known as "the Irish System." During the final stages of a sentence, Crofton's convicts were allowed to work without supervision and even to leave prison for short periods of time.

Gradually, American prisons passed from the control of religious leaders who sought to make "moral" citizens of inmates, to "progressive" people who believed that human society became better when scientific ideas were applied to problems like crime. Such a person was Zebulon Brockway.

At the National Prison Congress in 1870, Brockway argued that prisons should classify offenders by age, gender, and offense. He also called for use of *indeterminate* sentences.

Brockway said that judges should send people to jail for indeterminate periods of, say, five to 12 years. Inmates who cooperated with authorities would be released sooner than those who did not. Brockway believed that prisoners would behave and reform themselves in order to serve minimum sentences. Additionally, Brockway argued for aid and supervision of prisoners once they had been released back into society.

Part of the importance of the indeterminate sentence is that it takes power away from judges and puts it in the hands of prison professionals—wardens, parole boards, social workers, and counselors—people likely to have more contact with an inmate. Brockway's ideas were enlightened and effective, but the indeterminate sentence was not the perfect solution he hoped it would be.

Brockway failed to appreciate the difference between "behavior" and "reform." While many prisoners did work hard to get an early release, they did not necessarily reform. They simply learned to carefully follow prison rules. Once they were out, they returned to lives of crime.

The Industrial Prison

Prisons have had a kind of dual history. They have been places where inmates are made to work hard for the profit of others, and places where troublesome people are restrained.

At the Walnut Street Jail, prisoners were prevented from working at all because reformers thought they would become better people if they spent time alone and thought about their crimes. Later, however, this was found to be too harsh, and inmates were encouraged—even required—to work again.

Brockway's prison model stressed work, education, and job training so that prisoners would find jobs when they were released. Both the prisons and the states that operated them benefited by selling products manufactured at these factory prisons.

Unfortunately, however, shortly after the Civil War this practice began meeting with resistance from organized labor. American mechanics, welders, carpenters and workers from other skilled professions complained. They said that because prison products were produced with no labor costs, they could be sold more cheaply and were therefore hurting business.

Over time, this unfair competition created by prison labor led to the decline of production work in prisons. Eventually, most states passed laws forbidding sales of prison products on the open market. This meant that American prisons again became places where prisoners served out their terms in idleness.

During the first half of the 20th century, a period of relative calm descended on American prisons. The crime rate dipped in the 1930s as the nation struggled with the Great Depression. It also stayed relatively low through the 1940s, when many people were in the military service fighting World War II.

With the end of the war, however, crime and the prison population both increased. But instead of building new prisons, the courts attempted to fit more inmates into existing facilities. Many believed that criminal behavior could be treated and that more should be done to rehabilitate inmates. Efforts were made to provide prisoners with psychological counseling and job training. But these forward-looking efforts were irregular and expensive, and did not become successful or popular with the American public.

FIVE

A RAGE FOR REFORM

During the 1960s, many Americans became involved in the African-American struggle for racial equality. People of all races—but most especially black people—marched and protested against racism. An important result of the civil rights movement was that it succeeded in some of its goals. Poor people all over America began to realize that political activity was a tool that could change social conditions.

For example, many Americans believed that United States involvement in the Vietnam war was wrong. Efforts to persuade the government to withdraw from the fighting in that country had been either ignored or received with outright hostility. After years of struggling to make the government responsive to what the people wanted, those Americans demanding an end to the war began to be heard. When American troops were withdrawn from Vietnam in 1974, many believed that those who had agitated and demonstrated had gained their objective.

Civil rights activists and antiwar demonstrators often made public lists of demands for reforms. Soon prisoners in local, state and federal prisons and jails began demonstrating for reforms as well. They, too, often presented authorities with lists of demands for change.

But many Americans had become tired of change and demands for reforms. If laws are unjust they should be changed, they said.

Inmates of this Oklahoma prison stand outside under guard after a riot in which one dormitory was burned and several guards taken hostage.

Otherwise all laws should be obeyed. Activists, however, believed that no law would be changed until people could first be made to question it. The best way to get them to question it was to demonstrate against it.

San Quentin, 1967

While whites continued to dominate American life, African-Americans were the largest and most powerful group in most prisons. Racial tensions were high between the two groups—both in prisons and all over the country.

In 1967, a white guard in San Quentin

stuck his finger in a black prisoner's glass of milk. The result was a racial fight in which more than 1,000 inmates participated.

A few inmates, however, realized that racial fights were pointless. They argued that instead, the races should unite against the authorities in charge of the prison and demand some changes. These activists organized a "Unity Day." The purpose of Unity Day was to dramatize the need to struggle for prison reforms. A newspaper published at San Quentin warned of allowing prison authorities to "keep us at each others' throats. We want," said one story in the paper, "to crush this empire that has been built upon our suffering."

Soledad, 1970

In early 1970, prison authorities in California allowed a small group of African-American and white prisoners into the exercise yard of Soledad prison.

When a racial fight broke out, guards in a nearby tower opened fire. Three black prisoners were killed. This incident set off a period of intense racial hostility that was especially directed toward the white prison guards who had targeted the black prisoners. Eventually a white prison guard was overpowered, beaten and thrown to the ground from a third floor cell. He was killed.

George Jackson, an African-American political activist, was among those charged with the murder. Many inmates believed that Jackson was singled out by authorities because he was black.

Folsom

At Folsom prison, 2,000 inmates staged a non-violent strike that lasted three weeks. They sought to unite the races and demand improved prison conditions. Their manifesto claimed the right to "determine the direction of [our] own lives."

Among the demands of the striking prisoners was a call for ending the indeterminate sentence, "whereby a man can be warehoused indefinitely, rehabilitated or not." Strikers also demanded a popularly elected parole board instead of the politically appointed one.

Attica, 1971

In May 1971, inmates at Attica Prison in upstate New York issued a list of 29 demands. Once again, parole boards and sentencing policies were cited as sources of prisoner unhappiness. That September inmates rioted, taking 43 guards and prison employees hostage and seizing control of the prison. For several days, authorities negotiated with the prisoners.

But one of the guards beaten in the takeover died. This led the prisoners to demand amnesty, or freedom from prosecution for the man's death. Nelson Rockefeller, governor of New York, refused.

Ordered to retake the prison, state troopers and the National Guard stormed the strongholds, beating, wounding, and killing prisoners—most of whom were unarmed and tried to surrender. In the bloody aftermath, the Attica death toll was 43: 32 prisoners, and 11 employees of the prison.

Getting Tough On Crime

Back in 1968 there had been widespread rioting at the Democratic Convention in Chicago. Richard Nixon, the Republican candidate, was later elected president and built his political campaign on the issue of "law and order." Differences between political protest and street crime had become blurred.

Hundreds of other city and state politicians learned that elections could be won and lost on the crime issue. Political opponents who could be made to look "soft on crime" were easily defeated.

Has the 25-year-old policy of "getting tough on crime" lived up to expectations? Or has it helped create the current crisis in our criminal justice system?

Police departments have grown. Courtrooms and judges have been added. More prisons have been built. More arrests have been made. More criminals have been found guilty. Sentences have become longer. The cost to taxpayers has gone from millions of dollars to billions of dollars. According to an organization called the Sentencing Project, 1,000,100 men and women are currently in prison—twice as many people as there were in 1980.

Yet the crime rate has scarcely dipped at all. Violent crime—and, perhaps more significantly, the fear of violent crime—has reached undreamed of levels.

36 Hours In New Mexico, 1980

In February 1980, prisoners at a relatively new institution in Santa Fe, New Mexico, went on a bloodthirsty rampage. After gaining control of the prison, they brutally tortured and murdered 33 inmates believed to be snitches. Film of this riot was shown on television.

Americans were inclined to give up on the idea of the treatment model following the Attica revolt. But the New Mexico riot made people shiver with horror when they saw what prisoners were willing to do to each other. After the violence in New Mexico, the idea of rehabilitation became even less popular.

The New Mexico riot also signaled that times had changed since Attica. At Attica, prisoners had submitted a list of demands for change within the prison and rebelled when they received no response. Most of the violence and death at Attica had been caused by the National Guard and state troopers when they reestablished control over the prison. In New Mexico, the violence was caused by the inmates themselves.

The Santa Fe riot was like an explosion. Prisoners broke into the prison hospital and began taking the drugs. They murdered many fellow prisoners with blowtorches and shop tools. Only after their rage had been spent did the rioters issue a list of demands.

Among them was one that went to the heart of the matter: reduce prison overcrowding.

SIX

THE ERA OF OVERCROWDING

Between 1979 and 1984, 126 new prisons were built in the United States. Yet these prisons have not met the demand for more prison space. By 1985 our prisons were operating at between 106 and 121 percent of capacity.

On December 17, 1985, a group of prisoners seized control of the Oklahoma State Penitentiary in McAlester, Oklahoma. Although this uprising did not result in death or expensive destruction, a critical factor was that the prison population was 610 inmates, even though the prison was built to house 496. In other words, there were 114 more inmates than there should have been.

Three weeks later, inmates of West Virginia's Penitentiary at Moundsville used homemade weapons to take control of the prison. They forced guards to watch while they murdered three alleged snitches. Among the prisoners' demands was a smaller prison population. Once again the prison contained 100 more inmates than the number allowed by law. Sadly, three years before the Moundsville riot, the West Virginia Penitentiary had been placed under court order to improve conditions.

Prisons continue to be overcrowded to this day. In more than 40 states, courts have issued orders to reduce prison overcrowding. But the states have been slow to comply.

Frustrated by New York City's continuing violation of court-imposed limits on the numbers of allowed prisoners, New York Federal District Court

Many people believe that more criminals should be locked up for longer sentences to fight crime. But the capacity of our existing prisons is at the breaking point.

A deputy keeps an eye on a highway work gang near Arizona State Prison.

Judge Morris E. Lasker said that unless the city did something to reduce overcrowding, he would begin to charge the city $150 for each prisoner it held for more than one day in cells designed to "hold" but not "house" inmates.

Other states have actually been forced to pay prisoners sums of money for violating their constitutional right not to be subjected to "cruel and unusual punishment."

The Change In Sentencing

The indeterminate sentence encouraged judges to sentence convicted offenders to maximum and minimum terms. Under this method, a term of five to ten years could be minimized by good behavior.

People both inside and outside of prison recognized the weaknesses of indeterminate sentencing, however. Well-behaved and favored inmates were being released early, while political activists and those who were connected to trouble were being made to serve out their entire terms. In many cases, inmates who had been released too soon by parole boards committed new crimes and were sent back again.

The time had come for different sentencing policies. Congress and state legislatures heeded the call by fixing prison terms for certain offenses. This is called *determinate* sentencing. Judges were required to issue sentences that fell within certain guidelines. Prisons and parole boards were prevented from granting early releases to relieve the pressure on overcrowded prisons. Today, determinate sentences are widely used and have made prison overcrowding the norm—not the exception.

In prison there is very little privacy, and boredom is an inmate's constant companion.

The War On Drugs

The much talked about "war on drugs" has only intensified the public's outcry for harsher, longer sentences. The Anti-Drug Abuse Act was passed by Congress in 1986, making prison sentences for drug crimes longer and much more definite. As a result, judges have less say about prison terms in drug-related crimes. Sentence length is now fixed. A drug offender's sentence is tied to the amount and the kind of drug the offender had in his possession at the time of arrest.

In 1988, Congress stiffened these sentencing guidelines by doubling the penalties for anyone caught dealing near school yards, public swimming pools, video arcades, and other places frequented by young people. This means that cities and states sentencing drug offenders must issue the minimum sentences required by Congress. Some communities, however, hand out even longer prison terms for drug offenders. In fact, some states had very strict antidrug laws in place prior to federal laws.

For example, in 1986, police in Michigan stopped a car for running a red light. In the trunk of the driver's car police found 673 grams of cocaine— about a pound-and-a-half. Forty-five-year-old Ronald Harmelin received a life sentence.

Although Harmelin does not deny dealing cocaine, he feels the life sentence was too severe. The fact is that since Michigan has no death penalty, Harmelin is serving the maximum allowable prison term. Even if he had murdered someone—the police officer arresting him, for instance—he could not have been punished more severely in Michigan.

According to the *Detroit Free Press*, 123 people have received similar sentences in Michigan. About half of them were first offenders—they had no prior criminal convictions. Although the law was intended to put away major drug dealers, it has worked mostly against these medium-sized dealers. Federal Drug Enforcement Agency officers usually are the ones to arrest the truly big dealers, and even the new federal penalties are not as severe as those in Michigan. Under the new federal laws Harmelin would only have to serve ten years.

Although there continues to be a lot of emotionalism and very little agreement about sentence length for drug offenders, there has been no apparent let up in efforts to arrest those who use and sell drugs. In Los

A drug counseling session at New York State's "Shock Camp"—where inmates are treated as if they are in military boot camp. The regimented life is meant to keep these inmates from becoming recidivists.

Angeles, police have been making about 60,000 drug-related arrests a year for more than four years. They say they could arrest more offenders if there were more room in area prisons. As it is they limit the number of their arrests because jails, courts, and the parole system are already strained to the breaking point.

Lawbreakers And The Prison System

America is caught up in a vicious cycle. Fear of violence and crime creates an atmosphere of mistrust and blame. Politicians cry to "get tough on

Fear and Isolation

One of the best things to do is to try and forget about the outside world while doing time. My whole first year locked up I was totally hard timing and worrying about what was happening on the outside. What my wife was doing, whether we were going to be together, why I didn't get a letter from her that week, and just trying to predict things. It is best if you can just do your time, day by day, take care of yourself and let the outside world take care of itself...It's extremely hard, though, to keep your mind from wandering to life outside. You get a letter and something bad is happening with your family. It just drives you crazy...The most contact we have with the outside is mail. And even though you receive bad news at times, it is so important to get it...it is better to receive bad news instead of none at all. I've gone nuts when no mail came for weeks...

I am really thankful that I have no children out there. It's way too hard on the women, and from what I've seen your children coming to visit you here is hell. Watching them grow up in here, them asking when you're coming home and your wife having to do everything on her own. I'm sure that one of the main reasons that women leave their husbands in here is they are tired of being left out there and having to take care of the kids and their husbands in here....

—*David Kendig*

What A Prisoner Feels

Even though I don't want to be here, I have grown a lot in myself and this experience has given me time to really see where my priorities are. I believe if a man uses his time wisely he can get a lot out of it. Unfortunately, not many do, and just get used to this type of living.

What I am really trying not to do is get comfortable in here and get used to this. I can see how it would be very easy to...just want to be a tough guy around here, walking the walk and talking the talk. I did it for a while and found myself almost getting into trouble. I still do it at times...hiding from myself just to fit in and not be the odd man out. In prison you're surrounded by men trying to hide from themselves, people who are really damaged and hurting, and ready to fall into the victim, 'it's everybody's fault that I'm here but mine' role...there comes a point where we take responsibility for our actions. There are men in here who know that it is because of them they're in here, and it seems that they are the ones who try to rehabilitate themselves and stay out when they parole...

I know that there are no guarantees that I won't come back to prison. I will do everything in my power in here to help myself not come back.

—*David Kendig*

crime" and sometimes build their entire careers around putting people in prison. Politicians try to pressure judges and police to enforce the law and get the lawbreakers off the streets. But we need to ask ourselves what is being done in the way of preventative measures—positive programs to stop crime before it starts.

There are several approaches our society can consider. We can do a better job educating young people so that they will want to lead productive lives instead of destructive ones that end up behind bars. Creative alternatives to jail for first-time offenders —making criminals work off their crime, for instance—need to be explored and expanded. Law enforcement personnel and judges might do more to acquaint young people with the criminal justice system, and even interest them in the occupations that are a part of it.

We can create, staff, and support more halfway houses where both young and older offenders can be sent instead of to prison. We can use more electronic monitoring equipment to assist in supervising criminal offenders. And we must support equal opportunity in our cities and towns so that fewer people will decide to live outside the law, and the need for imprisonment will decline.

Glossary

APPEAL. A legal proceeding in which a higher court is asked to review the decision handed down by a lower court.

BANISHMENT. In centuries past, many criminals were sent away from their native lands and not allowed to return.

CRIMINAL JUSTICE SYSTEM. The social structure responsible for apprehending, bringing to trial, and acquitting or disciplining suspected criminal offenders.

CONJUGAL VISITS. Overnight visits by spouses to prison inmates.

DETERMINATE SENTENCE. A prison sentence of a length set by federal or state law which cannot be ignored by a judge.

DETERRENCE. A psychological fear of punishment that may keep some people from committing crimes.

DIVERSION. An opportunity for an accused person to avoid coming to trial by agreeing to terms specified by the court. For example: an agreement by an accused person to seek treatment for a drug or alcohol problem.

FELONY. A serious criminal offense as determined by law, usually carrying a sentence of one year or more.

INDETERMINATE SENTENCE. The practice of allowing judges to sentence offenders to indefinite periods of confinement. An indeterminate sentence allows parole and prison authorities to reduce the period of confinement in exchange for good behavior.

INMATES. People confined to prison by courts of law.

MISDEMEANOR. A minor criminal offense, usually carrying a sentence of one year or less.

PAROLE. The conditional release of an offender from prison. While on parole, an offender is supervised by a parole authority—either an officer or a group of officers.

PROBATION. The conditional freedom granted to an offender without serving time in jail. In exchange, the convicted person must meet certain conditions laid down by the court.

RECIDIVISM. The tendency of convicted offenders to return to crime and therefore end up in prison again and again.

REHABILITATION. The psychological restoring or curing of an offender so that he or she will cease engaging in criminal behavior.

SOLITARY CONFINEMENT. A form of punishment used by prisons in which an inmate is denied contact with others for a specified period of time.

Bibliography

Allen, Harry E. and Clifford E. Simonsen. *Corrections in America: An Introduction*. New York: Macmillan Publishing Company, 1986.

Bell, Malcolm. *The Turkey Shoot: Tracking the Attica Cover-up*. New York: Grove Press, 1985.

Bender, David L., and Bruno Leone. *The Death Penalty, Opposing Viewpoints Series*. San Diego, CA: Greenhaven Press, 1986.

Browning, Frank and John Gerassi. *The American Way of Crime*. New York: G.P. Putnam's Sons, 1980.

Clemmer, Donald. *The Prison Community*. New York: Holt, Rinehart, and Winston, 1968.

Hynes, Thomas J., Jr., ed. *Making Our Correctional System Work*. Lincolnwood, IL: National Textbook Company, 1989.

Reid, Sue Titus. *Criminal Justice: Procedures and Issues*. St. Paul, MN: West Publishing Company, 1987.

Silva, John W., ed. *An Introduction to Crime and Justice*. New York: MSS Information Corporation, 1973.

Sullivan, Larry, E. *The Prison Reform Movement: Forlorn Hope*. Boston: Twayne Publishers, 1990.

Toch, Hans, Kenneth Adams and Douglas J. Grant. Coping: *Maladaption in Prisons*. New Brunswick, NJ: Transactions Publishers, 1989.

Index

About The Author

Renardo Barden has edited a national sports magazine and written news and art criticism for several publications. To date he has published ten books and is at work on several others. Currently he lives in New York City, where he is involved in helping to curate a show of outdoor sculpture.

Picture Credits